FOUR ANCESTORS

STORIES, SONGS, AND POEMS FROM NATIVE NORTH AMERICA

TOLD BY JOSEPH BRUCHAC

PICTURES BY
S. S. BURRUS · JEFFREY CHAPMAN
MURV JACOB · DUKE SINE

BridgeWater Books

For my own grandparents:
Jesse and Marion, Joseph and Pauline
J.B.

10 9 8 7 6 5 4 3 2 1

Library of Congress Cataloging-in-Publication Data

Bruchac, Joseph, (date)
Four ancestors / by Joseph Bruchac; illustrated by S. S. Burrus . . . [et al].
p.   cm.
Summary: A collection of traditional Native American tales celebrating the wonder and mystery of the natural world, arranged under the categories "Fire," "Earth," "Water," and "Air."
ISBN 0-8167-3843-2
1. Indians of North America—Folklore.   2. Indian mythology.   3. Tales—North America.
[1. Indians of North America—Folklore.   2. Folklore—North America.]
I. Burrus, S. S.   II. Title.
E98.F6B894   1995   398.2'08997—dc20   [398.2]   95-15250

CONTENTS

FOUR ANCESTORS

The traditions of the many different Native American peoples all recognize the power and the importance of the four elements: fire, earth, water, and air. Stories and songs portray how very old those four elements are. Because Native American traditions view everything as alive, they see fire, earth, water, and air as living beings. As a sign of respect, a huge stone might be called Grandfather Rock. Or the earth, which, like a human mother, gives us everything we need, might be called Mother Earth.

In fact, it is often said that all things, including human beings themselves, were created by combining fire, earth, water, and air. So, in a very real sense, those elements are related to us. Just as we all have four grandparents, and our lives come from their lives, so we might describe fire and earth, water and air as our four ancestors.

Through stories and songs, poems and prayers, Native American tradition celebrates the wonder and mystery of the elements' creation. Unlike western science, which seeks to know and understand everything, Native American thought accepts that there are some things that people will never understand and do not need to know. Thus, the Creator is often referred to as The Great Mystery.

In this collection we pay tribute to the mystery and power of the natural world—and to our four ancestors. By honoring them, we hope to better understand ourselves and respect others.

FIRE

We see fire in many places. We see the Sun at the start of each day, carrying the fire of life up into the sky. At night we have the moon and the stars. And, like the people of long ago, we sit in front of a fireplace or around a campfire, enjoying the warmth of fires that we have made ourselves.

Fire helps us to survive when it grows so cold that the waters of the earth freeze. At that time of year we can see our own breath. It reminds us that we carry fire within us.

Fire gives us light. Many say that the sun's light is the first gift that was given to us by the Creator. "Greeting the Sun, a Maushop Story" reminds us that when the sun rises each morning, we must always remember to say words of greeting and thanks.

When the night comes, there is still light to be seen in the sky—the light of the moon. It is said by the Mohawk people in their thanksgiving address, "Thanks to Grandmother Moon" that the moon is the leader of women. She also governs the movement of the tides. By her changing face we measure time. Like that of a grandmother, her face is very kind as it looks down on us from the sky. The Pawnee people also see the moon as a grandmother. In their story "The Moon Basket," she gives the gifts of music and dance.

Another light, far, far above, is the light of the stars. The fiery shapes of the stars hold stories from the past. If we listen very closely, we may hear the stories, as told in "The Singing Stars," a Passamaquoddy poem. The Seneca story "The Three Hunters and the Great Bear" suggests that those starry lights are the campfires of the

hunters who travel across the sky.

One story told by the Chippewa describes a long time ago, before the people had fire, when thunderbirds collided with some stars. Those stars fell in pieces down onto the earth, becoming the first fireflies. To this day, Chippewa children sing the "Firefly Song" to the little pieces of a broken star. But although the fireflies brought the light of the sky down to the earth, they did not give warmth to the people. "How Coyote Stole Fire" tells how the animals got together and gave the people the warmth of fire.

We must always respect fire. If we do not, it may burn us. That is why the old people took care when they made campfires, clearing away the brush and leaves around the fire pit and placing stones around it in a circle so that the fire would not burn the forest. We must always be aware of the power of fire.

GREETING THE SUN, A MAUSHOP STORY

· WAMPANOAG ·

Long ago, as the Sun traveled across the sky, one of the first places he came to each morning was the land of the Wampanoag people. He would shine down on them, giving them warmth and light. But instead of thanking him for what he gave them, the Wampanoag people would look up into the sky, squint their eyes, and cover their faces with their hands.

"I do not like those little people making faces at me," said the Sun one day. "I will no longer visit their land. I will stay on the other side of the sky, where the people appreciate me."

So, when the next day came, the Sun did not rise up in the sky. Everything in the land of the Wampanoag people stayed dark and cold. The people became afraid and began to cry out.

"Someone help us," they cried. "Everything is dark. The Sun is missing. The world is going to end."

Maushop, the giant, had been sleeping, but the sound of many frightened voices woke him.

"Hunh," Maushop said. "It is dark."

Maushop stood up from the place where he had been sleeping on the beach, just below the great cliffs at Gay Head. He saw the little fires burning in the village of the Wampanoag people. Walking very carefully, so that he would not step on anyone in the darkness, Maushop went into the village.

"Maushop," the people cried. "You must help us. The Sun did not rise today. How can we survive without the Sun?"

"I will go and find the Sun," Maushop said.

Maushop turned and stepped into the ocean. He began to wade toward the east. His legs were so long that it took him only four steps to cross the ocean and four more steps to come to the other side of the world. There Maushop saw the Sun sitting in the middle of the sky and not moving.

"Older Brother," Maushop called up to the Sun, "why are you here? It is long past the time for you to bring the new day to the other side of the world. The people there are in darkness, and they are afraid."

"I am glad to see you, Younger Brother," said the Sun. "But as for those people on the other side of the world, I am not going there anymore. They never said thank you when I gave them light and warmth. All they did was squint their eyes and make ugly faces. I am going to stay here, where the people appreciate me."

Maushop turned and walked back across the ocean to the land of the Wampanoag people. He told the people what the Sun had said.

"If the Sun returns," the people promised, "we will greet him every morning. We will smile up at him and say thanks to him every day."

Maushop turned and walked back to the other side of the world.

"Older Brother," Maushop said to the Sun, "the people on my side of the world are sorry. They want you to return. They promise that they will greet you with smiles and words of thanks every morning."

"No," said the Sun. "I do not think they will remember what they promised. I will stay here. I will not move."

Maushop decided that he would have to show the Sun that the people really meant what they said. Maushop went to the spiders.

"My friends," said Maushop, "I need a big net. Will you weave it for me?"

"We will do as you ask," the spiders answered. They wove a huge net that was very strong.

Maushop picked up the net and went back to the Sun.

"Older Brother," Maushop said, "I want you to see that the people on the other side of the world meant what they said. You do not have to move. I will move you."

Then Maushop threw that great net over the Sun. He grabbed the

ends of the net in his hands, put it over his shoulder, and dragged the Sun back across the sky. Maushop was so strong that the Sun could not resist him.

As soon as they reached the land of the Wampanoags, the Sun heard voices calling up to him.

"Thank you," the voices called. "Thank you for bringing us light and warmth. Thank you for the gift of another day."

The Sun looked down at all of the people. They were not making ugly faces anymore. They were smiling up at him.

"Younger Brother," said the Sun to Maushop, "you were right. The people on this side of the world are happy to see me. From now on, as long as they greet me this way, I will come to their land every day."

So it is to this day. Sometimes, when the light is just right in the sky, you can still see pieces of that net, made long ago by the spiders, hanging down from the Sun. When the Wampanoag people see that, they remember how Maushop helped them. And they remember that as long as they greet and thank the Sun, he will return with his gifts of light and warmth every morning.

THANKS TO GRANDMOTHER MOON

· MOHAWK ·

Now, again, we put our minds together.
We give thanks and greeting
to our oldest grandmother, the Moon.
She is the one who lights
the nighttime skies.
Our grandmother is the leader
of women all over the world.
She is the one who governs
the motions of the ocean tides.
By her changing face
we measure time.
It is Moon, our grandmother,
who watches over the arrival
of children here on earth.
With one mind, we send greetings
and thanks to our grandmother, Moon.

THE MOON BASKET

· PAWNEE ·

When the world was first made, two people were created out of mud. They were First Boy and First Girl. The earth was in darkness then, and First Boy was given a bow and arrows and told to go hunting. The animal he killed would determine how much light there would be. Many animals ran by him: a black deer, a gray elk, and a white antelope. But he did not shoot them. Then a buffalo that was half white and half black ran by. First Boy shot that buffalo. Ever since then, we have light half the time and dark half the time.

First Boy and First Girl made themselves a rough little lodge of grass and lived there together for some time. They gathered plants or hunted in the forest. They were happy during the days, when the sky was filled with the light of the sun. But they were not happy when night came, because then the sky was filled with darkness.

First Boy and First Girl did not want to go outside because it was so dark. They sat in their little lodge in the darkness. They had no songs to sing, and they did not know what dancing was. So they could not enjoy themselves.

One night, they heard the sound of drumming. Then they heard voices singing. They had never heard singing before, and they listened closely. Those voices were strong and beautiful.

First Boy and First Girl followed the sound of the voices until they came to a clearing. In that clearing was a field of tall plants they had never seen before. It was the first corn. In the center of the clearing was a big lodge made of long poles and covered with buffalo skin.

An old woman with a shining face greeted them.

"I am Moon Woman," she said. "Come into my lodge."

First Boy and First Girl went into the lodge of Moon Woman. Many girls were dancing inside. They were Moon Woman's daughters, the Stars. First Boy and First Girl had never seen anyone dancing before.

There was singing inside the lodge, too. Four old men were leading the singing. They were the four powers of the sky: Wind, Cloud, Lightning, and Thunder.

"Watch our dance," said Moon Woman. "Then you will know how to do the dance of the Stars. Listen to the songs, and you will know how to sing them."

First Boy and First Girl watched closely so that they would remember how to do this thing called dancing. They listened closely to the songs so they would remember how to sing. And all the while, as the powers of the sky sang and the stars danced, the brightness of the Moon filled the lodge with light.

Moon Woman picked up a beautiful basket made of long, slender willow twigs woven together. Inside that basket was a beautiful ball of white light. Moon Woman called First Girl to her.

"Daughter," Moon Woman said, "look at this basket. See how it is made, and you will be able to make baskets of your own."

Then Moon Woman showed First Girl how to bend the willow twigs and weave them together. She showed her how to line the basket with mud so that it could be used to carry hot coals without burning or water without leaking. First Girl paid close attention so that she would be able to make her own moon baskets.

"The mud in this basket makes it more like the earth. Such baskets stand for all of creation."

While Moon Woman showed First Girl how to make baskets, the four old men showed First Boy how their lodge was made. He, too, paid attention so that he would remember.

"You do not have to live in a small grass hut," they told him. "See how this lodge is made. See how we cover it with buffalo hide. This is the kind of lodge that you and the people to come should make. Those plants that grow outside our lodge will also be yours. They are corn.

Corn will help feed the people to come."

When Moon Woman was done teaching First Girl how to make baskets, she led both children outside. She held up her moon basket, and the Moon rose up into the sky. Moon Woman's daughters, the Stars, came out of the lodge. Wind, Cloud, Lightning, and Thunder sang and the star girls danced up into the sky. Now the night sky was bright and filled with light.

"Tirawa, our great Creator, wants things to be this way," said Moon Woman. "Now the night sky will be filled with the light of my daughters. You will see my face in the ball of light that is the Moon. You can see the dance of life in the movement of the Moon and the Stars. Always remember to watch us as we dance across the sky. The moon basket will remind you of the things we have taught you."

Then Moon Woman rose up into the sky, and her face could be seen in the bright Moon.

First Boy and First Girl remembered the things Moon Woman taught them. They sang the songs they had learned, and they danced the dance of the Stars. They danced to thank Tirawa, the Creator, for filling the night sky with light. First Boy made a lodge like the lodge of the four powers of the sky. First Girl made a moon basket of willow twigs and lined it with clay. And they taught those things to the people who came after them.

So it is that the Pawnee people learned long ago how to make the moon basket. So they were given the gift of corn and taught how to make fine lodges. So it is that they learned how to sing and how to dance to thank the Moon and the Stars.

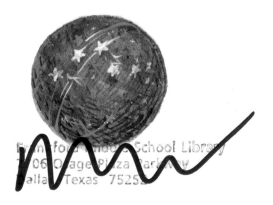

THE SINGING STARS

· PASSAMAQUODDY ·

We are the Stars who sing.
We sing with our light.
We are the birds of fire
who fly across the sky land.
Each of our lights is a Star.

We sing on the road of the spirits,
the road of The Great Mystery.
Among us there are three hunters
who follow the tracks of the bear.
There was never a time
when they were not hunting.
We look upon the mountains.
Our song is a song of the mountains.

THE THREE HUNTERS AND THE GREAT BEAR

· SENECA ·

Long ago there was a little village. The people in that village lived very well until a strange thing happened. The deer disappeared from the forest, and the fish vanished from the streams. Whenever the men of the village tried to hunt, they found no game.

One day, two hunters went out from the village. One of them went up on a hill to look around while the other followed the trail. Suddenly the one on the trail fell into a hole that had not been there before.

"Where did this hole come from?" called the hunter who had fallen.

The hunter who was up on the hilltop looked down and grew afraid. "That is no ordinary hole," he called back. "Come up here and see."

The first hunter scrambled out of the hole and climbed to the hilltop. When he looked down, he, too, became afraid. The hole into which he had fallen was the paw print of a giant bear.

The two hunters hurried back to the village to tell their story.

"This is why the game has vanished," one of the elders said. "This is why the fish are gone from the streams. This giant bear has eaten all the fish and all the animals."

"We must build fires around the village," said another of the elders. "Now that all the other food is gone, the great bear will come after us."

In that same village, there were three brothers who were the greatest of all the hunters. Whenever they went out hunting with their little dog, they always brought back game. The first brother had such keen eyes that he never lost the trail. The second brother was so strong

21

that he could carry back anything they caught. The third brother was so good at throwing a spear that he never missed. But he was also one of the laziest men in the village.

"We will go out and get that giant bear," said the first brother.

"We will not stop until we have caught it," said the second.

"But first we will take a nap," said the third.

"No," said his brothers, "we will go right now." And even though the lazy hunter protested, they set off on the trail of the giant bear.

The first brother, whose eyes were keen, quickly found the trail. The second brother was close behind him, carrying a big pot and a load of firewood so that they could cook some of the meat from the bear after they caught it. Their little dog was close beside them, sniffing the air. The third brother hung back.

"Brothers," he said, "let us stop and rest for a while."

Just then, the little dog began to bark. It ran into the thick brush by the side of the trail. As soon as it did, the giant bear ran out the other side. It was afraid of that little dog's bark.

"We see you," shouted the first brother.

"We are going to catch you," shouted the second brother.

"Don't run so fast," shouted the third brother.

Then the three brothers ran after the bear as their little dog nipped at its heels. The bear ran through the forest, but they stayed close behind. It ran up the hills, and they still stayed close behind. Then it came to a tall mountain and began to climb. It went higher and higher, but the brothers still followed.

The third hunter, though, was tired of running. "Brothers," he said, "I have hurt my foot and can run no farther. Each of you must grab one end of my spear so that I can sit on it while you carry me."

His two brothers did as he asked. On and on they went as the bear climbed higher and higher up the mountain. It was growing dark, and the third brother was becoming so heavy that they were beginning to fall behind.

"Brothers," said the lazy hunter, "put me down. My foot feels much better now."

So the brothers put him down. Because he had rested, the third brother ran ahead. When he caught up with the bear, he drew back his spear and threw it, killing the giant bear.

The three brothers were very happy. They made a fire, cooked up some of the bear meat, and began to eat. Then the first brother looked around. There were lights all around them in the darkness. Then he looked down.

"Brothers," he said, "we are up in the sky."

The brothers looked around. It was true. That giant bear had fled up into the sky land, and they had followed it up among the stars.

Suddenly they heard their little dog barking. The giant bear had come back to life and was running away. They took up the chase again.

If you look up into the night sky, you can still see the three hunters following the great bear, circling around the sky. They are the stars some call the Big Dipper and others call Ursa Major, the Great Bear. The three stars behind the bear are the hunters, and the faint star with them is their dog. Every year, in the autumn, the Great Bear turns upside down. When Seneca children see that, they say, "Look, the lazy hunter has killed the great bear again."

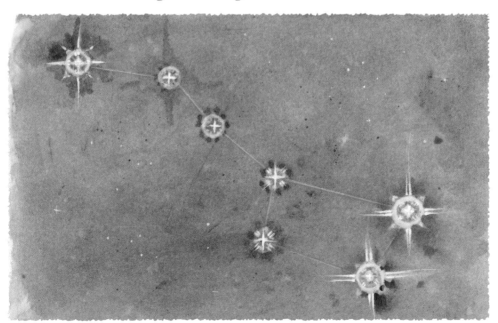

FIREFLY SONG

· CHIPPEWA ·

Wau-wau-tay-see
White fire insect
Wau-wau-tay-see
White fire insect
E mow e shin
Tahe bwau ne baun-e wee!
Give me light
before I sleep!
Be-eghaun be-eghaun-ewee!
Before I sleep, before I sleep!
Wau-wau-tay see
White fire insect
Wau-wau-tay-see
White fire insect
Was sa koon ain je gun.
Light me with your bright white flame.
Was sa koon ain je gun.
Light me with your bright white flame.

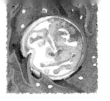

HOW COYOTE STOLE FIRE

· COLVILLE ·

Long ago, the people had no fire. All the fire in the world was held by the Fire Keepers, powerful beings who lived in a crater on top of a mountain. These beings, called Skookums, guarded the fire and shared it with no one.

In the winter, the people were very cold. The animals had fur coats to keep them warm, but they saw how the people were suffering and took pity on them.

"We must help these people," Coyote said. The other animals agreed. So Coyote chose four other animals to help him: Cougar, Squirrel, Antelope, and Frog. He told each of them to hide and wait for him to come down the mountain with fire. Then Coyote crept up to the crater where the Skookums stood guard.

There were four Fire Keepers. Three would sleep while one guarded their precious fire. Coyote watched them take turns and saw that the smallest Skookum was not as mindful as the others.

Coyote watched and waited until the smallest Skookum stood guard. Then he crept closer. Closer and closer he came. Suddenly he grabbed a burning stick and ran away with it!

The four Skookums followed Coyote across the snow, breathing fire. The First Skookum grabbed at Coyote with its burning claws but only brushed the end of his tail. His tail turned black and is black to this day.

Coyote came to the place where Cougar was hiding in the trees. He threw the burning stick to Cougar, and Cougar ran. The Skookums were close behind. The Second Skookum grabbed at Cougar with its

burning claws but only brushed the tip of his tail. It, too, turned black.

When Cougar reached the plains, he tossed the stick to Antelope. The Third Skookum was so close that it grabbed Antelope's long tail and burned it off. To this day, Antelope has almost no tail. But Antelope leaped away and ran until he came to the river where Frog waited.

By now all that was left was a glowing ember. Frog swallowed it. The Fourth Skookum leaped at Frog and grabbed his tail, but Frog jumped and twisted and his tail broke off. To this day, Frog has no tail.

Then Frog dived into the river, where the Skookums could not follow. He swam across the river and crawled out on the other side. He spit the ember into the wood of that tree.

Then Coyote went to the people.

"Little brothers and sisters," Coyote said, "we have brought you fire. It was not easy for us, but we have done it because we pitied you. The fire is hidden in those trees down by the river. If you take dry sticks from those trees and rub them together, sparks will come out. Those sparks will grow into flames. Then you will have fire to warm you and to cook your food. We know that you will continue to hunt us, but show us respect and remember that we have brought you this gift."

So it was that Coyote and the other animals brought fire to the people. And the people, who show respect to the animals, have never forgotten that great gift.

EARTH

To the Native American peoples, earth is never seen as just dirt. Instead, earth is described as our Mother and seen as the source and support of all life. Whether it is the soil beneath our feet, the rocks, the great mountains, or the clay that can be shaped into useful objects, earth in all its forms is recognized to be alive. Further, as the Navajo "Song of the Earth" reminds us, this earth is a glorious place, and we must never forget to appreciate and be grateful for its beauty.

Animals take part in many stories of earth's creation. It is believed not only that animals are very wise, but that they care about human beings. That is why they act as companions to people and even allow human beings to hunt them. Thus, it should come as no surprise that the Osage tale "How the Earth Began" has a great elk at its center.

Before there was anything else on earth, there were the stones. To many Native peoples, the stones are seen as being no different from other living things. They are alive, and because they are so ancient, the stones are respectfully referred to as Grandfather, as in the story of "Wihio and Grandfather Rock." Geologists tell us that the stones were formed from molten lava long ago. It is interesting that the Lakota story of creation begins with "Inyan, the Rock," who is formed out of fire.

If the earth and the stones are alive, then the great mountains are also full of life. Because mountains are so tall, it is said that they can see much of the earth around them. It is still a common Native American practice to climb a mountain and enjoy the beautiful view. This is even done in the nighttime, as the Abenaki song "The Shining

Mountain" describes. We know how alive a volcano can be, breathing forth volcanic ash or great flows of lava. Is it any wonder that a mountain might also be seen as a monster or a danger to the people, as in the Nisqually story "Tacobud, the Mountain That Ate People"?

Of all the things that are made of earth, clay is the most responsive to human beings. We can pick it up and shape it with our hands. We can make useful objects out of it, including the shapes of people, as is done in "Clay Old Woman and Clay Old Man," the Cochiti Pueblo story. The relationship between Native people and clay is a very, very ancient one. Pieces of clay pots have been found in the remains of villages that existed thousands of years ago. Like her ancestors, young Mary Grey must remember to give thanks to the riverbank for the clay she gathers in "Talking to the Clay."

Whether it is the soil or stones, great mountains or yielding clay, we are never far from the earth. It supports all our lives. When we understand this, we may begin, as Native peoples have always done, to appreciate the many gifts of the earth.

SONG OF THE EARTH

· NAVAJO ·

Daltso hozhoni
Daltso hozho'ka'
Daltso hozhoni
All is beautiful
All is beautiful indeed
All is beautiful.

Now Mother Earth
And Father Sky
Meet each other, join each other,
Companions always to each other.
All is beautiful
All is beautiful indeed
All is beautiful.

The night of darkness
And the dawn of light
Meet each other, join each other,
Companions always to each other.
All is beautiful
All is beautiful indeed
All is beautiful.

Now the white corn
And the yellow corn

Meet each other, join each other,
Companions always to each other.
All is beautiful
All is beautiful indeed
All is beautiful.

Now Life That Never Ends
And Happiness of All Things
Meet each other, join each other,
Companions always to each other.
All is beautiful
All is beautiful indeed
All is beautiful.
Daltso hozhoni
Daltso hozho'ka'
Daltso hozhoni.

HOW THE EARTH BEGAN

· OSAGE ·

Long ago, before there was the Earth, the people and the animals lived together among the stars. But there were so many people and animals that the sky land became crowded. They needed another place to live.

"We must do something," the animals said to the people. "Let us go and ask the Creator for help."

So the animals and the people went to Wah-Kon-Dah, the giver of life. Wah-Kon-Dah listened carefully to their request.

"Creator," they said, "we are crowded here in the stars. And what will happen as more of our children are born? There will be nowhere for them to stand. We need a place with more room. Can you help us?"

"Your request is a good one," Wah-Kon-Dah said. "Go below to Honga, the Earth. She will be your mother and take care of you. But you will have to respect and care for her. You will have to remember you are all related. All living things are brothers and sisters. You must try to live together in peace."

The animals and people were pleased to hear this. They all agreed with Wah-Kon-Dah's words and said they would try to remember them.

Then the animals sent messengers down to the Earth. Soon the messengers came back.

"Honga is covered by water," they said. "Someone will have to find dry land for us to live on."

So the Water Strider and the Water Beetle went down to look for dry land, but they could not find it. The Leech looked for land and

33

could not find it. To this day, Water Strider, Water Beetle, and Leech still live in the water.

At last the mighty Elk said that he would try. He dived out of the sky land into the water far below and began to swim. As he swam, he bellowed to the four directions, and the Four Winds began to blow. They pushed the water up to form the first clouds.

Now the Elk could see the brown Earth lifting up out of the water. He climbed up onto the brown Earth and began to roll with joy. As he rolled, a plant grew wherever a hair fell from his coat. He rolled and rolled until the new Earth was covered with grass and bushes and trees.

Then the people and the animals came down to the new Earth. Everyone found their own special place and their own job to do. Among them were the Osage people, who remembered what they had been told by Wah-Kon-Dah, the Creator. The people must care for Honga, the Sacred One, the Earth. It would be their job to help keep the harmony.

So the Osage people lived as caretakers, never taking too much, always showing love and respect for all life on the sacred Earth. They remembered that all living things are sisters and brothers. They remembered that it was their responsibility to keep the balance. And so they live to this day.

WIHIO AND GRANDFATHER ROCK

· CHEYENNE ·

Wihio was out wandering around. It had been a long time since he had eaten anything, and he was very hungry. As he walked along, he saw a hill and decided he would climb it to see if he could spot any game. When he got to the top and looked around, he still could see nothing. But there was a great boulder on top of that hill. Wihio spoke to it.

"Grandfather," said Wihio, "you are old and have great power. I would like you to help me."

Then Wihio took his flint knife and placed it on the ground in front of the big stone.

"Grandfather," Wihio said, "this knife is a gift to you. Please help me find some food."

As Wihio went back down the hill, he saw something in the valley below him. It was a cow buffalo that had just died.

"Aha," Wihio said. "This is a gift to me from Grandfather Rock."

Wihio ran down and looked at the cow buffalo. "There is enough meat to keep me fed for a week," he said. "Now I just have to cut it up so I can carry it back to my lodge."

But Wihio had given his flint knife to Grandfather Rock. He decided to pretend that he had not given it as a gift but had just forgotten it.

"Now where did I put my knife?" Wihio said. "That's right, I left it up on the hill. I will go back and get it."

Wihio ran up the hill again. His fine flint knife was right where he had left it when he gave it to Grandfather Rock.

"You do not need this knife," Wihio said to the great boulder. "You are just a big stone."

Wihio picked up the knife and ran back down to the place in the valley where he had seen the dead buffalo. But when he got there, all that was left were old, dry bones.

Wihio ran back up to the hilltop where the great boulder still sat.

"Grandfather," Wihio said, "I was only joking. Here, this knife is yours. Just give me back that buffalo."

Then Wihio placed his knife next to the big rock.

"Here, Grandfather," Wihio said. "Now I am going to go get my buffalo."

But when Wihio ran back down into the valley, even the dried-up bones were gone.

Wihio went back up to the hilltop. The great rock still sat there, but now Wihio's fine flint knife was gone, too. Once again, Wihio had been too clever for his own good.

So Wihio got nothing to eat, and he went on his way even hungrier than before.

INYAN, THE ROCK

· LAKOTA ·

Inyan, the Rock,
had no beginning,
for he was when
there was no other.

His spirit
was the Great Mystery
and he was the first of all.
He was soft and shapeless
like a cloud then,
but he had all the powers
and was everywhere.

Inyan, the Rock,
longed to use his powers,
but he could not do so,
for there was no other.
So he took from himself
to make a great disk
whose edge is where
there can be no beyond.
This disk he named
Maka, the Earth.

To create the Earth,
Rock took from himself
so much that he shrank,
became hard, and lost his power.
And that which flowed
from Inyan, the Rock,
became blue waters,
the waters of Earth.

Thus, in the beginning
there was Inyan, the Rock,
Maka, the Earth,
and the waters,
all of which are the world.

THE SHINING MOUNTAIN

· ABENAKI ·

Let us go together
up the shining mountain.

Let us sit and watch
Peguis, the Sun,
the Day Traveler,
go down in beauty.

Nanibonsad, the Moon,
she who walks all the night,
will climb into the sky land.

The Alakwesak,
the far-off beings overhead,
the little stars, will follow.

Now we hear
the drum of Thunder,
now sparks fly from
the pipe of Lightning.

Now Great Owl sings,
all must sleep,
all must sleep,
the Alakwesak and their chief
are in flight across the sky.

But, though our bodies
urge us toward sleep,
we sit in beauty
upon the shining mountain.

TACOBUD, THE MOUNTAIN THAT ATE PEOPLE

· NISQUALLY ·

Long ago, the mountains were people. Each of the peaks of the Ho-had-hun, the Olympic Range, was once a person. Among them was the great one called Tacobud. Once she had lived with the other mountains, but as they grew larger, Tacobud became irritable. She decided there was not enough room.

"I will move away," she said. "Things are too crowded here. I will go toward the rising sun, where the people have no mountains. I will go and take salmon and berries with me, so the people will have plenty to eat."

So Tacobud did as she said. She crossed over to the other side of Puget Sound and found a new place to stand, where there were no other mountains. She began to grow taller and taller until she became a giant mountain. On her slopes were great herds of animals. Salmon swam in the streams at her base, and there were berry bushes everywhere on her sides. People came and settled around Tacobud, and they were grateful for everything she gave them.

But as Tacobud lived there, she began to change. Some say it was because she grew lonely, for there were no other mountains close to her. As she grew lonelier, she became more angry. No longer was she kind to the many people who came and settled around her. She no longer liked the human beings who climbed her slopes to hunt elk and deer. She became a terrible monster.

Whenever people climbed up Tacobud, she would open her mouth and suck them in. The people begged the mountain to be kind, but Tacobud did not listen. She just swallowed them up. Warriors went to

43

challenge her. But Tacobud was so large that she swallowed them, too. As Tacobud grew larger, her hunger grew greater and greater. The people were very afraid.

One day, Fox came to help the people. "What is wrong?" she asked.

"It is Tacobud," said the people. "She is swallowing up everyone. No one can defeat her."

"I will do what I can," said Fox.

The Fox twisted together bark to make a very strong rope. She tied that rope about herself and fastened one end firmly to the earth. Then she went to Tacobud.

"Great One," she said, "I challenge you to a contest. Let us see which of us can suck the other one into her stomach."

"No one can defeat me," roared the mountain. "I will swallow you."

"That may be so," said Fox. "You go first."

Tacobud took a deep breath and began to suck. She sucked so hard that the bushes all around her mouth were sucked in. But Fox, who was fastened to the earth, did not move.

Tacobud tried again. This time she sucked so hard that she sucked in the trees on her slopes. Fox still did not move.

Now Tacobud tried even harder. She sucked so hard that rocks and boulders rolled up the slopes and into her mouth. But Fox remained where she stood, her rope holding her tight to the earth.

Tacobud became very angry. She took another deep breath, and another and another. Then she breathed in so hard that she burst inside. The monster died and rivers of red lava flowed down her sides like blood.

Fox said, "Tacobud is no longer a monster. The channels that have been shaped on her sides will become rivers full of fish. The people will be safe. Because Tacobud became so angry and tried to eat everyone, she will no longer be a person. From now on Tacobud will only be a mountain."

And that is how it is to this day.

CLAY OLD WOMAN AND CLAY OLD MAN

· COCHITI PUEBLO ·

Long ago, people did not know how to make pots. So Grandmother Spider made Clay Old Woman and Clay Old Man, and she sent them to the Pueblos.

Clay Old Woman and Clay Old Man walked into the plaza. Clay Old Woman brought clay with her. She brought sand and water and began to mix them together. When she was finished she rolled the clay into a ball.

As she worked, Clay Old Man danced and sang, "This is how pots will be made."

All the people gathered around them. They watched as Clay Old Woman began to make long coils from the ball of clay. She rolled the clay between the palms of her hands. Then she began to build a pot with those coils. She finished one pot and then another. When she had finished enough pots, she carefully piled wood around them and made a fire. She piled wood on top of the pots. People watched this, too. They saw how the pots hardened in the fire. All this time Clay Old Man kept singing and dancing.

When the fire had burned out and the pots were cool, Clay Old Woman took them out and placed them on the ground. The people admired what Clay Old Woman had made. But although those pots looked good, they were not strong enough to last. Clay Old Man knew this. He came dancing up to the pots. Then, to everyone's surprise, he kicked them over. The pots all broke into small pieces. Clay Old Woman chased Clay Old Man around the plaza with a stick, but she did not catch him. As he ran, he still sang his song.

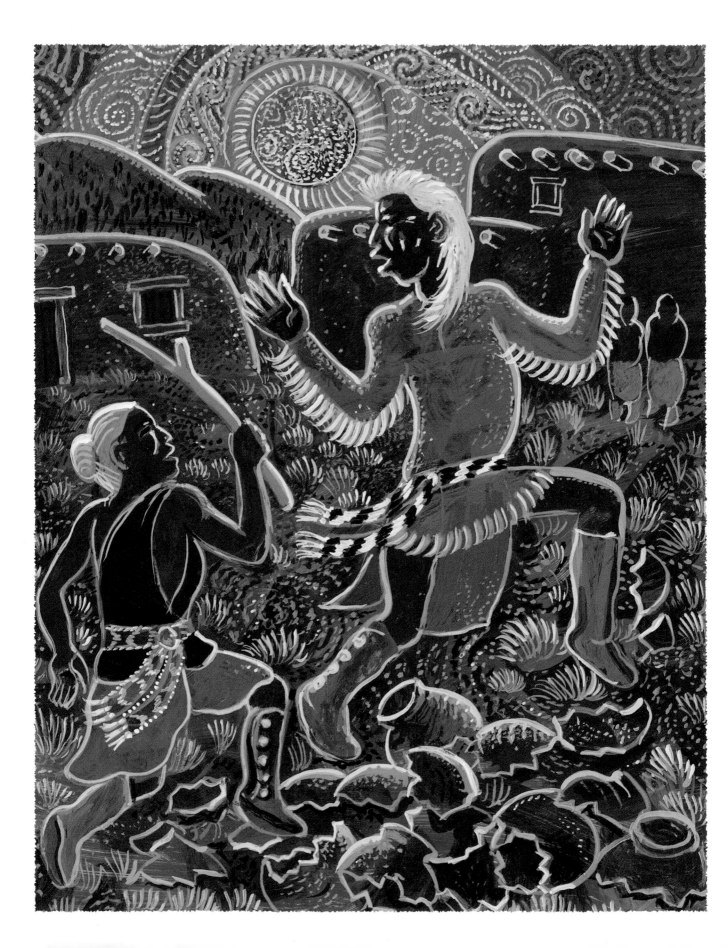

This is how pots will be made.
This is how pots will be made.

Clay Old Woman finally stopped chasing Clay Old Man. She went back to her broken pots and picked up the pieces. She broke them into even smaller pieces and ground them up. Then she mixed those ground-up pieces in with the rest of her clay. Now the pots that would be made would be strong. They would last.

Ever since then, pieces of old broken pots have been used in making new pots. And so it was that people learned that unless something is done the proper way, it will not be good. It might look good, but it would not last.

Then Clay Old Woman divided up the clay. She gave a piece of it to everyone in the village.

"If you need more clay," Clay Old Woman said, "you will find me by the river."

Then Clay Old Woman and Clay Old Man departed from the Pueblos, but they left behind the gift of pottery. Now the people had pots that they could use to carry water and store food. Those pots made their lives much better.

To this day, people who make pots go to the river where Clay Old Woman can be found in the banks of clay. As they gather the clay, they thank her. Often they leave presents for Clay Old Woman. And as the people coil their pots and fire them, they sing songs, just as they were taught to do by Clay Old Woman and Clay Old Man. To this day, that is how the people make pots.

TALKING TO THE CLAY

· CATAWBA ·

Mary Grey walked down to the river, carrying her bucket. It was a warm spring day, and the South Carolina hills were bright with sunlight. As Mary walked, she watched for that same yellow color in the riverbank. That color of the sun would show her that she had found the clay she was looking for.

Usually Mary's grandmother went with her to gather clay. But today Mary was going alone for the first time.

"I'm a little tired," Grandma Rose said, handing Mary the plastic bucket. "You are old enough to do this by yourself."

Mary had been surprised, but she was determined to do a good job. She realized that her grandmother was testing her.

After all, Mary said to herself, *I am ten years old. I'm almost a grown-up!*

Mary kept her eyes open, looking for clay. She could go to the spot her grandmother had shown her, but she wanted to find her own place. She wanted to hear the clay speak to her.

Mary was proud of the fact that her people still talked to the clay. A lot of the other people in the Southeast had given up making pottery more than two hundred years ago. It was easier to use the metal pots that the Europeans brought them. But the Catawba didn't forget. They used metal pots, but they still made clay ones. "You don't have to give up the good old things to accept the good new ones," Grandma said. Remembering that clay was alive and remembering to talk to it was one of those good old things.

Mary thought about how good the clay always felt as she worked it

with her fingers. That was how you found the sticks and stones that had to be taken out before you could make anything. The clay felt so alive! She thought it was happy to be cleaned like that.

Mary had been only three years old when Grandma Rose started teaching her how to talk to the clay. Her grandmother had just finished making a small round pot. It hadn't yet been put into the fire to harden. Her grandmother put the pot in Mary's hands.

"You feel how this pot is breathing?" Grandma Rose said.

"I feel it breathing," Mary said. And she *had* felt it moving in her hands, had felt that it was alive.

A kingfisher darted down from a tree branch and dived into the river just ahead of her. As Mary's eyes followed the bird, she saw a yellow gleam on the bank. Holding the pail tight, she scrambled down the bank and looked. It was clay. She reached out and pulled a little free and squeezed it. It made a round ball in her palm.

Mary put down her bucket and reached into her pocket. She took out a stone that was not a stone. Her uncle, who knew a lot about such things, had told her it was actually a fossil tooth. It came from a big animal called a mastodon, which lived long ago. Mary had found that tooth when she was out walking. It was her favorite thing.

"Clay," Mary said, "I'm glad you let me find you. I want to give this to you. I want you to be my friend for a long, long time."

She dug a hole at the base of the clay bank and placed the stone tooth into it. Then she stood and listened. It seemed as if she could hear a voice, soft and flowing like the sound of the river behind her.

"Thank you," she said. Then she began to fill her bucket with clay.

WATER

Although non-Native peoples often have taken water for granted, the Native peoples of North America regard water as one of the great gifts from our Creator. Water is truly all around us. It is carried in the clouds above us, and it falls as rain. Rivers flow across and shape the face of the land, and oceans surround it.

The desert peoples of the Southwest, in particular, know how important rain is. The Zuni story "The Cloud-Swallower Giant," for example, tells how heroic twins defeat a terrible giant who threatens to swallow all the rain in the clouds. Many songs and dances thank the rain and to ask it to return. It is regarded as a blessing that helps the crops grow. The "Papago Rain Song" celebrates this life-sustaining bounty.

Snow is another form that water can take. When we have too much snow, however, it can make life difficult. The tale "Gluskabe and the Snow Bird" explains how the good giant Gluskabe kept the Snow Bird from making too much snow. This story is a favorite of Penobscot children. It also contains a lesson about jealousy and pride.

Saying a prayer of thanks each morning before taking the first drink of water is a common Native practice. Although it is not safe to do so now, only a generation ago people could drink water directly from most streams and rivers. Water was even thought to have healing properties. Among the Cherokee people, one of the oldest healing ceremonies is called Going to the Water, and it involves going down to the river and drinking its water at dawn.

Rivers are of deep importance to Native peoples. They not only provide drinking water but are also a source of food and means of transport. Thus, as the Maliseet tale "Aglabem's Dam" emphasizes, the rivers were meant to be shared.

The waters of life run through our bodies in our blood, which is as salty as the oceans. The edges of the ocean are full of life, and because of the tides, many kinds of food can be gathered at the beaches. The story "Raven and the Tides" reminds people to be grateful for the gifts they receive from the ocean. In a similar way, the Yurok story "How the Prairie Became Ocean" shows us just how much the ocean offers. The events described in the story seem to tell of a giant earthquake that helped people by bestowing upon them the good things brought by the ocean.

The image of North America for most Native peoples is that of a great turtle floating in a huge sea. In many ways, whether in the form of rain or snow, rivers or great oceans, water is never far from the minds of Native peoples.

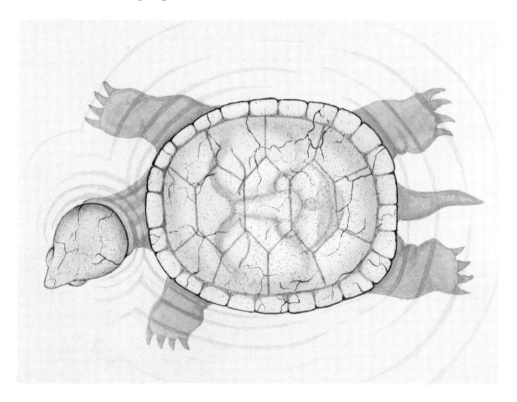

THE CLOUD-SWALLOWER GIANT

· ZUNI ·

Long ago, a great giant lived among the cliffs to the north. The people called him Haki Suto, which means "topknot," because his thick black hair was braided and tied up on top of his head. Haki Suto was a monster who ate human beings. He was also known as the Cloud Swallower because he was so tall, he caught the clouds to drink the rain from them.

Because Haki Suto had captured all of the clouds, rain no longer fell on the land. The rivers and wells dried up. The corn began to die in the fields. Without the clouds, the land was never shaded, so things were always hot. The people knew they would not be able to survive without the blessing of rain.

Many men went up into the mountains to try to free the clouds and defeat the giant. But none of them ever came back. When they reached the place where Haki Suto sat, he would kick them off the cliff with his great leg. Then Haki Suto's children, the monster birds who lived in the cliffs, would eat them. The valley below was filled with the dry bones of people killed by Haki Suto.

One day the warrior twins, Ahaiyuta and Matsailema, heard about what was happening. It was their job to fight the monsters who threatened the land and the people.

"We must go and destroy Haki Suto," said Ahaiyuta.

"You are right, brother," said Matsailema.

So they set out on the trail that led to the northern cliffs. But before they had gotten very far, they heard a small voice calling to them.

"Grandchildren," that voice said. "I know where you are going. Let me help you."

The warrior twins looked down at the ground. There, balanced on top of a tall blade of grass, was Spider Grandmother.

"Grandmother," said Ahaiyuta, "we are glad to see you."

"I am glad to see you, grandsons. But you are on a dangerous trail. It leads to the Cloud Swallower's place."

"We know this," said Matsailema. "We are going to destroy him."

"That is good," Spider Grandmother said. "But the Cloud Swallower will try to trick you. He will pretend he is asleep. When you speak to him, he will not even open his eyes. He will tell you he is too tired to stand up and fight you. He will tell you to pass under his legs, which stretch over the trail. But when you try, he will kick you off the cliff. He has done that to many people."

"What can we do, Grandmother?" said Ahaiyuta.

"I will go ahead of you and make it so that he does not see you," said Spider Grandmother. "Wait until the sun is in the middle of the sky before you follow me."

Spider Grandmother hurried up the trail until she came to the narrow place where the great giant sat. His legs were bigger around than the biggest trees. He sat with his back against the canyon in which he kept all the clouds that he had captured. Spider Grandmother could hear the clouds crying. Whenever Haki Suto was thirsty, he would reach back, grab a cloud, and squeeze all of the rain from it into his mouth.

Spider Grandmother was so small that Haki Suto did not see her. She crawled up the cliff and then let herself down by a line of silk onto his thick topknot of hair. She sat there and waited.

Soon the sun was in the middle of the sky, and she could hear the warrior twins coming up the trail. Haki Suto, the Cloud Swallower, heard them, too. He closed his eyes and pretended to sleep.

Then Spider Grandmother let herself down onto his eyebrows and began to spin her web over his eyes. Haki Suto felt this, but thought it was only a gnat buzzing around his face. He did not try to brush it away because he was pretending to sleep.

Now the warrior twins came to the place Haki Suto sat.

"We have come to free the clouds," shouted Ahaiyuta.

"Stand up so we can fight you," shouted Matsailema.

"I am too old and weak to stand up," said Haki Suto. "You can set the clouds free if you want to. Just go under my legs."

The warrior twins began to go under the giant's legs. Haki Suto tried to open his eyes to see them, so he could kick them off the cliff. But Spider Grandmother's web held his eyes shut.

"Where are you?" Haki Suto cried. He struck at the warrior twins and kicked his feet. But he could not see, so he could not hit them.

"We are here," shouted Ahaiyuta.

"No, we are here," shouted Matsailema.

They led the giant to the edge of the cliff. Then they pushed him over.

Haki Suto fell to the bottom. He fell so hard that his feet drove into the ground, and he was turned into a pillar of stone. His children, the monster birds, flew down from the cliffs. Ahaiyuta and Matsailema grabbed them, twisted their necks, and squeezed them so that they became smaller. Today those birds are the owls and the falcons that still live in the cliffs.

Then the warrior twins set the clouds free from the place Haki Suto had kept them captive. The clouds drifted up into the sky and floated over the land of the people. The rain again began to fall, and the people sang with joy.

So it was that Haki Suto, the Cloud Swallower, was defeated long ago. And to this day, the Zuni people sing songs of joy and thanksgiving to the clouds that bring the rain.

PAPAGO RAIN SONG

· PAPAGO ·

Clouds stand in the east; they are approaching.
It rains in the distance.
Now it rains here and thunder rolls.

The green rock mountains thunder with clouds.
With this thunder Akim village is shaking.
The water will come down the arroyo
And I will float on the water.
Then the corn will ripen in the fields.

Close to the west, the great ocean is singing.
Waves are rolling toward me, covered with clouds.
Even here I can hear the sound.
Earth shakes beneath me; I hear the deep rumbling.

A cloud atop Evergreen Mountain is singing.
A cloud atop Evergreen Mountain stands still.
Up there it is raining and thundering.
Here, too, it is raining and raining.
Under the mountain corn tassels are shaking.
Under the mountain the horns of the child corn glisten.

GLUSKABE AND THE SNOW BIRD

· PENOBSCOT ·

Wawogit Gluskabe. Here camps my story of Gluskabe, the good giant who always tried to help the people long ago.

In the old days, Skunk was one of the most beautiful of the animals. His pure white fur, as white as new snow, was long and silky. All of the animals admired him.

But Skunk was not happy. He saw how the people praised Gluskabe for doing great things.

"I, too, want to do great things," Skunk said. So he went to Gluskabe.

"Gluskabe," said Skunk, "I would like to travel with you. You know that I am a good cook. If you let me come with you, I will prepare all your meals."

Gluskabe knew this was so, and Gluskabe liked to eat good food. "My friend," Gluskabe said, "you may travel with me."

For a time, things went well. Skunk cooked all the meals, and the two of them sat together in Gluskabe's lodge. Then, one day, a messenger came from the north.

"Great One," the messenger said, "I have come to ask you for help. The snow has been falling for so long that we are unable to hunt, and we are running out of food. The snow is so deep that we are unable to gather firewood to heat our lodges. If you do not help us, we will surely die."

"I must go and speak to the Snow Bird," Gluskabe said. "He is the one who controls the snow." Gluskabe began to make ready for his journey.

Skunk packed up his cooking gear, but Gluskabe stopped him.

"My small friend," Gluskabe said, "you cannot go on this journey with me. The snow will be deep, and you will not be able to walk through it."

"I will be fine," said Skunk. "If the snow gets deep, I will just walk in your footprints."

"Are you sure this is what you wish to do? This may be a difficult journey."

"I am sure," said Skunk. So Gluskabe allowed him to come along.

As they walked toward the north, the snow grew deeper and deeper. At first it was not hard for Skunk, but soon he found himself jumping from one of Gluskabe's footprints to the next. This was not easy, because Gluskabe was so large that his footprints were far apart. Skunk began to get angry at Gluskabe. He forgot that it was his own idea to come along.

At last they came to the hilltop where a great white bird stood. As he spread his wings, snowflakes fell from them.

"Hello, Grandfather," said Gluskabe.

"Ah, Gluskabe," said the Snow Bird. "Why have you come here?"

"Grandfather, it is good that you make the snow. The snow cleans our land. It covers the plants so that they will not freeze when the weather grows cold. When the snow melts, it fills the rivers and the lakes. But now there is too much snow. If it continues to fall like this, the people will not be able to live."

Gluskabe bent down and pulled up Skunk, who was half-frozen, out of the deep snow. "See how hard it is for my little brother here?"

The Snow Bird nodded. "I see."

"Grandfather," said Gluskabe, "the snow should not fall without stopping. You should not make every snowfall a deep one. Sometimes the snow should be heavy and sometimes it should be light. Then, when the winter is over, you should close your wings. Only open them in the time between first frost and last frost."

"I shall do as you say," said the Snow Bird. He folded his wings, and the snow stopped. To this day, snow only falls for part of the year.

The snow was melting as they walked back to Gluskabe's lodge, and Skunk found it easier to walk. But he was still angry. He wanted to do something by himself that everyone would remember.

As they walked along, they passed another hilltop. A great bird stood on top of it. He held his wings open wide and light streamed out.

"Who is that?" asked Skunk.

"That is the Day Eagle," said Gluskabe. "While his wings are open, it is day all over the world. When he closes them, it will be night."

Skunk saw that this was so. The Day Eagle was just closing his wings and the evening was beginning. Soon it was dark, and they made camp for the night.

Gluskabe fell asleep, but Skunk stayed awake. He took a big ball of rawhide twine and went to the place the Day Eagle stood. Skunk bound the great bird's wings so tightly with the twine that he would not be able to open them, no matter how hard he tried. Then Skunk sneaked back to camp and pretended to sleep.

When the next day came, there was no daylight. The birds and the animals wandered about in the dark. The people were afraid. But Skunk was not afraid. He laughed at the confusion he had caused.

Gluskabe found his way to the Day Eagle's hilltop.

"Who did this to you, Grandfather?" he asked.

"It was the white one who travels with you," said the Day Eagle.

Gluskabe tried to untie the knots Skunk had made. They were very tight, so tight that Gluskabe could not untie them all. He was only able to free one of the Day Eagle's wings. To this day, the Day Eagle can only open one wing. That is why half the world is always dark, while the other half is light. The Day Eagle must keep turning around on his hilltop to share his light with the world.

Gluskabe went back to camp, where Skunk was still pretending to sleep.

"I know what you have done," Gluskabe said. He took the ashes from the fire and emptied them over Skunk so that his white coat

became all black. With his fingers, he drew two white stripes down Skunk's back to remind Skunk of how beautiful he once had been.

"Now everyone will remember what you have done," Gluskabe said. He blew smoke on Skunk, and Skunk became bad-smelling. "Now none of the people will want to be with you."

Ever since then, Skunk seldom comes out until it is dark. It is not just that he is ashamed of his sooty coat; he also fears that the Day Eagle will seek revenge for what he did long ago. Skunk also sleeps during most of the winter, for he remembers how hard it was to walk through that deep snow long ago.

To this day, the Snow Bird is careful to do as Gluskabe told him. Sometimes when the snow falls there is much snow, and sometimes there is only a little. But the snow no longer falls without stopping. The Snow Bird always closes his wings at the end of winter. He does not open them again until long after summer ends.

So it is to this day.

SONG FOR GOING TO THE WATER

· CHEROKEE ·

If your heart is not well,
If your spirit is not well,
These words may help you.

Wake in the hour
Just before dawn.
Wake in the hours
Before first light.
Wake when the animals of the night
Have ended their songs,
When the animals of the day
Have not yet begun their songs.

Walk without words.
Follow the path
That leads to the stream.

Then, as the first light
Touches the stream,
Bend to the water,
Speak these words:

"Long Person, I come to ask your help."

Then hold up
A cup of that water
And drink the dawn.

AGLABEM'S DAM

· MALISEET ·

Here lives my story. A great monster named Aglabem decided that all of the water in the world belonged to him. So he made a great dam in the place the rivers began and kept back all of the water. The rivers no longer flowed. The lakes went dry. All over the world, people began to die of thirst.

Aglabem was as large as a mountain. He had a mouth big enough to swallow a whole village. His fingers and toes were as long and as yellow as the roots of the birch trees. He was too great a monster for the people to fight, so they sent a messenger to him, begging for water.

"I cannot give you any water," Aglabem said in a deep voice. "I need all of this water so that I can lie in it. The water belongs to *Aglabem, Aglabem, Aglabem.*"

All that he gave the messenger was a cup of mud.

The messenger went back to the people and told them what Aglabem had said.

"Now we will all die," the people said. "We cannot live without water."

They began to pray for help. Kitchee Manido, the Creator, heard their prayers and sent his helper, the great giant Kuloskap, to see what the people wanted.

"Great One," the people said to Kuloskap, "the monster Aglabem has taken all of the water in the world. Without water we will die."

"I will help you," said Kuloskap. "I will go and speak to Aglabem." Then he set out toward the north, where Aglabem kept all the water.

As soon as Kuloskap left, some of the people began to talk of what they would do if the river water was returned to them.

65

"I would swim like a beaver," said one person.

"I would drink forever like a fish," said another.

"I would dive in like a frog," said a third person.

"I would float around like a turtle," said yet another.

Kuloskap walked and walked until he came to the place Aglabem kept all of the water. Aglabem was floating in that water.

"The people need water," said Kuloskap.

"All of this water is mine," said Aglabem in his deep voice. "It all belongs to *Aglabem, Aglabem, Aglabem.*"

"No," said Kuloskap, "the water is meant to be shared."

"I will not share it," croaked the monster. "It all belongs to *Aglabem, Aglabem, Aglabem.*"

Then Aglabem stood up, ready to fight Kuloskap. But Kuloskap grabbed hold of a great poplar tree and threw it down onto Aglabem's dam, freeing the water. That great tree turned into the St. Johns River. Its many branches became the streams flowing into the river. Its wide leaves became the ponds that feed those streams.

As the water of the river went by the place the thirsty people lived, many of them leaped into the river. The one who wanted to swim like a beaver became a beaver. The one who wanted to drink forever like a fish became a fish. The one who wanted to dive in like a frog became a spotted frog. And the one who wanted to float around like a turtle became a turtle. That is why to this day the river is filled with so many fish and spotted frogs and turtles and beavers.

Then Kuloskap picked up Aglabem and squeezed him so that his back became bent and his eyes and his cheeks bulged out. He squeezed him so hard that the monster grew smaller and smaller until he became what he is today—a bullfrog.

Then Kuloskap threw him into the river. "This water is meant to be shared by everyone," said Kuloskap, "so you can stay in it."

To this day, Aglabem, the bullfrog, jumps into the water whenever he hears anyone coming, for fear it might be Kuloskap. But at night he still tries to claim that all the water is his. If you are quiet, you may hear him calling out his name: "*Aglabem, Aglabem, Aglabem.*"

RAVEN AND THE TIDES

· TSHIMSHIAN ·

We-gyet, the Raven, was walking along the beach. He was hungry, but he could see nothing to eat. In those days, the tides did not go in and out as they do today. Sometimes the water would stay up on the beach for a long time, and there would be nothing for the people to eat.

That was how it was on that day. The tide was so high and the ocean water was so deep that We-gyet could not get clams or seaweed or any of the delicious things that could be found when the tide went out.

"This is not good," We-gyet said. "I will go and see what is causing this."

Then We-gyet put on his cloak of black feathers and began to fly above the beach. As he flew, he looked down and saw a long line connected to the water. It was the tide line, which let the water go out or held it when it came back in. We-gyet followed that tide line.

At last We-gyet came to the end of the line. It led up the beach to a house made of cedar planks, with a huge pile of clamshells next to it. We-gyet landed and took off his cloak of feathers. Now he looked just like a person again.

We-gyet walked up to the open door of that house and looked inside. A strong old woman sat there, holding the tide line in her hand. She was Tide Woman. Tide Woman's house was full of food from the ocean. She had clams and scallops, barnacles and sea urchins, crabs and seaweed. It made We-gyet even more hungry when he saw all that good food. Because the door was open, We-gyet walked inside.

"Hello, Grandmother," We-gyet said.

Tide Woman said nothing back to him. So We-gyet sat down.

"You have a lot of food to eat here, Grandmother," We-gyet said.

But the old woman did not offer We-gyet anything to eat.

"Grandmother," We-gyet said, "why don't you let go of the tide line? Then other people can go and gather food."

But Tide Woman only held on to the tide line more firmly.

I see that I will have to trick her, We-gyet thought. Then he smiled. "I am not hungry myself," We-gyet said. "I recently finished eating many clams just up the beach."

Tide Woman looked out the door. "How could that be?" she said.

"Just up the beach, your line is broken." We-gyet said. "The tide went out, and there are big clams everywhere."

The old woman stood up to look out the door. "How could that be?" she said again.

"Just go and look," said We-gyet.

As Tide Woman stepped out the door, We-gyet tripped her. She dropped the tide line, and the tide rushed out. All along the beach, good things from the ocean were exposed. And all along the beach, the people rushed out to gather food.

The old woman tried to grab the tide line again, but We-gyet threw sand into her eyes so that she could not see. Then he walked down to the beach and began to gather food himself. He gathered clams and scallops and crabs, and he ate until he could eat no more. Finally, when his belly was full, he walked back up the beach to the old woman's house.

"We-gyet," Tide Woman said, "I cannot see, but I know that you are the one who tricked me. Heal me and I will do whatever you want."

"You must promise to let go of the tide line two times every day," We-gyet said. "Then the people and I will always be able to gather enough food."

"I will do as you ask," said Tide Woman.

Then We-gyet washed the sand from her eyes and put the tide line back into her hands. Because Tide Woman is old and forgetful, she doesn't always let the tide go out at the same times each day. But she does remember her promise to We-gyet. And so it is that the tide goes in and out two times every day.

HOW THE PRAIRIE BECAME OCEAN

· YUROK ·

Long ago, when there were no people, the ocean was a treeless plain. Thunder stood and looked over the land. He knew that soon people would be there.

"How will the people be able to live?" Thunder turned to his companion, Earthquake. "What do you think?" Thunder asked. "Should we place water here?"

Earthquake thought. "I believe we should do that," he said. "Far from here, at the end of the land, there is water. Salmon are swimming there."

So Earthquake and Water Panther went to the end of the land, where there was ocean. They picked up two big abalone shells and filled the shells with salt water. Then they carried the shells back to Thunder.

Earthquake began to walk around. As he walked, the ground sank beneath him. Water Panther filled the sunken ground with the salt water.

Now there was ocean where there had only been a treeless plain. Thunder rolled over the mountains and bent the trees down so they would grow on the land. Seals and salmon and whales swam through gullies made by the sinking land.

Beside the ocean, the land rose up into hills and animals came down from the mountains—deer, elk, foxes, and rabbits.

"Now this will be a good place for the people to live," Thunder said.

"This is a good place," Earthquake agreed. "Let us live here, too."

And so, to this day, Thunder and Earthquake live there, near the place they made the land into ocean for the people.

AIR

Each breath we take depends upon the existence of something we cannot see—the air. Without that air, we could not live. Whether air is in the form of the breath that fills our lungs or the living breath of our planet, the wind that crosses the land, we are always in its presence. And our words—our stories and our songs—are carried on the air.

Native Americans have always observed how the wind brings the life-giving clouds and the rain. In many traditions, the wind is embodied in the form of a great bird. The Micmac tale "The Bird Whose Wings Made the Wind" illustrates the importance of the wind in maintaining the natural balance. Native peoples have special words of thanks to say to the wind, which is seen as the source of breath and life. Songs, such as the "Wind Song" of the desert-dwelling Pima people, speak of the living, singing wind.

Native peoples see clearly how breath and life are connected. As explained in the Navajo tale "The Whirlwind Within," our fingerprints give visible evidence of the inner wind that is the source of our lives. The whirlwind is sometimes seen as a living person. The story "How Saynday Tried to Marry Whirlwind Girl" is both an amusing tale and a teaching story that reminds Kiowa children that we need to respect the whirlwind.

Traditional Native beliefs hold that the sky is alive and close to the people. According to the Snohomish story "How the People Pushed Up the Sky," the sky was at one time so close that people had to bend over to walk beneath it. It was only through great cooperation that they were able to push the sky higher. People would also look up at the sky and

imagine it filled with songs that would bring the people together, such as "A Song of the Sky" from the Tshimshian of the far northwestern coast.

Native American peoples appreciate how music and storytelling are carried on the breath of our voices. Birds also have such voices, as we are reminded by the Navajo "Bluebird Song from the Night Chant." Singing and telling stories are thought to be as natural as breathing. When the Inuit people speak of how songs are made, they describe it as breath and spirit being put together. That breath we all share is the breath of the living wind, the breath of the sky, the breath of stories.

THE BIRD WHOSE WINGS MADE THE WIND

· MICMAC ·

There was a family that lived in a birch-bark *wikuom* by the ocean. In that family there was a mother and a father and several children. Each day they would go down to gather food in the shallow water, where they could find clams and mussels and lobsters and eels.

One day, though, the wind began to blow. It blew so hard that great waves washed over the rocks, and it was not safe for them to gather food.

"Soon this wind will stop," said the father of the family. "We will wait here in the *wikuom* until it grows calm."

But the wind did not stop. It blew steadily, night and day. It went on this way until the family ran out of food and began to starve.

"You must go and see if you can find some food," said the mother of the family to her husband.

"My wife," he said, "you are right." He picked up his spear and tied to it a strong line made of basswood twine. That way, if he threw his spear at something in the water, he could pull the spear back in.

Then, bowing his head against the wind, the man crawled out of the *wikuom* and made his way down to the shore. The wind blew so hard that he could barely stand, but he continued forward, leaning on his spear. When he came to a point of land that thrust out into the ocean, he thought he could see something far out on the rocks. He continued on, making his way forward so he could see what was out there.

At last the man reached a big stone, where he could find shelter from the wind. As he crouched behind it, he looked out to see what it

was that stood on the farthest point of land just ahead of him.

What he saw surprised him. It was a giant bird. As he flapped his wings, the wind blew. And because the bird flapped his wings without stopping, the wind also blew without stopping.

So, the man said to himself, "This is the bird that causes the storm wind. I must find some way to make him stop."

Then the man took a deep breath and called out as loudly as he could to the great bird.

"Grandfather," the man shouted. "Grandfather, listen to me."

The Wind Bird stopped and looked around.

"Who is calling to me?" said the Wind Bird.

The man came out from behind the rock and walked up to the Wind Bird.

"Grandfather," said the man. "I came out here because you are so cold."

"I am not cold," said the Wind Bird.

"Grandfather," said the man, "you are cold. Do you not feel cold out here?"

"Perhaps I am cold," said the Wind Bird.

"Yes," said the man, "you are very cold. I came out here to help you get back to the shore, where it is warm. I have come to carry you."

"That is good," said the Wind Bird, and he allowed the man to pick him up.

The man began to make his way back to the shore with the Wind Bird on his back. He jumped from rock to rock and waded through the shallow places. It was easy to do this now, for with no wind the sea had grown very calm. However, just as he reached the shore, the man pretended to stumble. He dropped the Wind Bird so that he fell onto one of his wings.

"Grandfather," said the man, "I am sorry. I have broken your wing."

"My wing does not feel broken," said the Wind Bird. "It doesn't hurt at all."

"Grandfather," said the man, "your wing is broken. I must use my line to bind it to your body so that it will heal properly."

The man began to wrap the line around the Wind Bird. He wrapped it so tightly that the Wind Bird was unable to move either of his wings. Then he placed the Wind Bird in a sheltered place among the rocks on the shore.

"This is good, Grandfather," said the man. "Now I will leave you here so that your wing can heal. I will bring you food now and then."

The man returned to his *wikuom* with a smile on his face. He called his wife and their children. All of them went down to the shore, where they gathered many shellfish and lobsters and crabs and eels. Then they had a great feast. When they had finished eating, the man took some of the food to the Wind Bird.

"Grandson," the Wind Bird said, "I think my wing is better now."

"No," said the man, "it is not yet healed. It will take a long time for it to be better."

When the sun rose the next day, the man and his family went down to the shore to gather food. However, the sea and the beach were all covered with foam. The man and his family could not see into the water, and they could not find any food. Each day the foam grew worse.

"My husband," said the woman, "it is the wind that keeps the water clean. You must untie the Wind Bird."

So the man went back to the Wind Bird.

"Grandfather," the man said, "your wing is healed."

"Grandson," said the Wind Bird, "that is good."

Then the man untied the Wind Bird. But, as he did so, he said, "Grandfather, you must be very careful or this wing may break again. From now on, you must flap your wings more gently, and you must rest them from time to time."

"I will do so," said the Wind Bird. And so it is that to this day the wind does not blow all of the time.

WIND SONG

· PIMA ·

The wind now begins to sing.
The wind now begins to sing.
The land before me stretches away,
stretches away before me.

Now the house of wind is thundering.
Now the house of wind is thundering.
As I go roaring over the land,
the land is covered with thunder.

And now, above the windy mountains,
now above the windy mountains,
the many-legged wind comes running.
the wind comes running to me.

The Black Snake Wind comes to me.
The Black Snake Wind comes to me,
comes and wraps itself about me,
comes running here with its songs.

THE WHIRLWIND WITHIN

· NAVAJO ·

In those first days, there was no language. All the people and all the animals understood one another without speaking. First Man and First Woman and all the others who lived back then did not have to speak. They wandered about, going wherever they looked, only following their eyes.

Then they encountered Wind. Wind spoke to them. "You do not know where you are going," Wind said. "You do not yet know things. But I know things. I go all over the earth, and I know all about it. I have given you life."

Then First Man and First Woman spoke to Wind. "Thank you," they said. "How will we know things?"

Then Wind became words. Wind became language. Wind moved into their ears, and they heard words spoken. So the ears of people are round like the Wind, which swirled within them and gave them words.

Now people could listen to the words of others. Because they could hear what others said to them, some people could be leaders. Because they spoke through Wind, those who led would always be influenced by the Wind, who gave life to everyone.

So it is that to this day, when anyone speaks for the people, they speak on behalf of Wind. They speak for that one who guided the ancestors. Whenever we breathe, it is with the help of Wind. When we speak or we sing, it is through Wind. The whirlwind is within us and will always be beside us. And because it was the whirlwind that gave us breath, there are round swirling lines on the ends of the fingers and the toes of all human beings. They remind us of the whirlwind of life within us all.

HOW SAYNDAY TRIED TO MARRY WHIRLWIND GIRL

· KIOWA ·

Saynday was coming along. That is how every story about Saynday begins, and that is how this story begins, too. It was not that Saynday was looking for trouble, but he was about to find it.

As Saynday was coming along, he saw a beautiful young woman. He had never seen anyone like her before. She was spinning around and dancing, and the buckskin fringe on her dress swirled as she danced.

"Ah," Saynday said. "Who are you? Where did you come from? I have never seen you before."

"My name is Mankiah, the Whirlwind," said the young woman as she continued dancing. "When the season of great heat comes, I always come here out of the west and the south. Have you forgotten who I am?"

Indeed, Saynday had forgotten. Long ago, he had tried to make the first horse but had not succeeded. So he threw away what he made, and it turned into the Whirlwind.

"You are very good-looking," Saynday said. "And I am very good-looking, too. I think you and I should get married."

"I do not think that you are good-looking," Whirlwind Girl said as she kept on dancing. "And I do not think we should get married."

"You should get married while you are young," Saynday said. "Since I am here now and I want to marry you, that is a good reason for you to marry me."

"You might not enjoy being married to me," Whirlwind Girl said. "People say it is not easy to live with me."

"Ah," Saynday said, "people say it is not easy to live with me

either. It is clear that we should get married. Let's get married right now."

Whirlwind Girl was getting tired of Saynday, but she could see that he would not go away.

"I cannot marry anyone unless they can dance," she said as she danced around and around.

"That is good," said Saynday. "I am a very good dancer."

"Then come and dance with me," said Whirlwind Girl.

That was all that Saynday needed to hear. He closed his eyes and ran toward Whirlwind Girl to embrace her. But Whirlwind Girl was ready. She grabbed Saynday and spun him around and around. The air filled with dust and dry leaves as she flung him high into the air and carried him over the plain. Saynday was so dizzy that he could not even cry out. Then she dropped him way over on the other side of the river, far from his home.

Saynday stood up and shook the dust and leaves and sticks from his hair and his clothes. He could see Whirlwind Girl dancing away in the distance, but he did not try to follow her.

"I am afraid that I was just too good a dancer for her," Saynday said. Then he went on his way in the other direction.

HOW THE PEOPLE PUSHED UP THE SKY

· SNOHOMISH ·

When Dohkwibuhch, the Changer, made the world, he began in the east and moved toward the west. As the Changer came across the land, he gave a different language to each group of people he created.

When Dohkwibuhch reached Whulge, the great saltwater bay now called Puget Sound, he stopped. Whulge was a beautiful place, and so the Changer decided to go no farther. He decided he had done all that was needed to be done. However, he still had many languages left over. So he scattered them all around that place. That is why, to this day, there are so many different languages there.

Although the many Native peoples spoke many different languages, they were not happy with one thing: When Dohkwibuhch decided that his work was finished, he had not yet raised up the sky. The sky was so low that the people had to bend over as they walked. If they stood up straight, they would hit their heads on the sky. If they could jump high, they could leap right into the sky land. If they were not able to jump high, they could just climb a tree into the sky land. When they wanted to return to the earth, all they had to do was jump back or climb down a tree.

Finally, the wise elders of all the different peoples got together. They decided that the sky should be lifted higher, so things would be better for everyone.

"We can make poles from the tallest fir trees and use them to push up the sky," one of the elders said.

"We can do this if everyone works together," another of the elders said.

"That is good," said yet another elder. "To do this we will all have

to push together at the same time. But our people all speak different languages. What can we use as a signal?"

"Let us make up a new word," said a fourth elder. "Let us agree that *Ya-Hoh* will mean 'lift together' in all of our languages."

So it was decided. All of the people agreed. The wise elders would shout that word all at one time. When the shout of *"Ya-hoh!"* was heard, then everyone would push together and lift up the sky.

Everyone got ready. They cut poles from the tallest fir trees and held them so that they all touched the sky. Not only the people did this. The birds and the animals were also tired of always hitting their heads on the sky. They, too, held poles to push the sky up higher.

Then the signal was given. *"Ya-hoh!"* shouted the elders.

Everyone pushed. All the different peoples, all the birds, and all the animals pushed up the sky. Now it was higher, as high as the tallest trees, but it was not high enough.

"Ya-hoh!" the elders shouted a second time. Again everyone pushed. Now the sky was high above the trees, but it was not yet high enough.

"Ya-hoh!" the elders shouted a third time. And then a fourth time they shouted, *"Ya-hoh."* Now the sky was so high that no one would ever bump his or her head on it again. It was so high that no one could ever again climb up into the sky land. All the different peoples and the birds and the animals had pushed up the sky, and it is there to this day.

Some people, though, had not heard about the decision of the wise elders to lift up the sky. Those were the people and the animals who had climbed up or jumped up into the sky land before the sky was lifted; they were turned into stars. Among them were three hunters and their little dog, who were all chasing an elk. Today, they make up the stars of the Big Dipper.

To this day, whenever the people are working hard or want to lift something together, they still say, *"Ya-hoh!"* just as those wise elders did long ago. And it is still true that when people work together, they can do almost anything, even lift up the sky.

A SONG OF THE SKY

· TSHIMSHIAN ·

I will now sing
a song of the Sky.
It is the song
of those who are tired.

The owl flies down
in slow, slow circles.
The salmon pauses
in the swift current.

While above them
always looking down
is the great wide face
of Sky above us.

I walk by the river
where the water rushes
down into the whirlpools,
the talking water.

The voice of the water
here is swift. It sounds
as if it is in a hurry,
yet the song of the Sky is slow.

The owl and the salmon
call me to stop,
to rest here beneath
the wide Father Sky.

So, beside the river,
I sit down and look up,
and the song that I sing
is a song of the Sky.

BLUEBIRD SONG FROM THE NIGHT CHANT

· NAVAJO ·

Tsolgali, the bluebird, has a voice.
Tsolgali, the bluebird, has a voice.
Just at dawn Tsolgali calls.
Tsolgali has a voice.

Tsolgali, the bluebird, has a voice.
His voice is sweet,
his voice is sweet,
it flows with gladness.
Tsolgali calls.
Tsolgali calls.

Tsolgali, the bluebird, has a voice.
Tsolgali, the bluebird, has a voice.
Just at sunset Tsolgali calls.
Tsolgali has a voice.

Tsolgali, the bluebird, has a voice.
His voice is sweet,
his voice is sweet,
it flows with gladness.
Tsolgali calls.
Tsolgali calls.

HOW SONGS ARE MADE

· INUIT ·

Songs are born in that stillness
when everyone tries
to think of nothing but beautiful things.
Then they take shape
in the minds of people
and rise up like bubbles
from deep in the sea,
bubbles seeking the air
so that they can burst.
That is how songs are made.

THE GIFT OF STORIES, THE GIFT OF BREATH

· ABENAKI ·

"Where do stories come from, Grampa?"

The little girl looked up at her grandfather. Her face was very serious.

"Well," Grampa Obomsawin said, his brown face opening into a smile, "the ones you hear from me, I tell them to you."

"That's not what I mean, Grampa," the little girl said, pulling hard on her braid.

"Now, what do you mean, Cecile?" Grampa Obomsawin said, leaning forward to show he was really listening.

"I mean before you knew them."

"Some people say that the stories come from the earth, from the stones themselves. A long, long time ago there were a few people who were patient enough to listen to the stones. Every time they heard a new story, they gave the stones a gift of some kind, maybe some beads or a nice arrowhead. And so the stones kept telling more stories to them. Those folks learned those stories and then told them to the other people. That might be so, but I don't think that's the whole story."

Grampa Obomsawin paused. Cecile knew it was her turn to say something, to show she'd been listening. "What is the whole story, Grampa?"

"The whole story is that the stories are all around us. They're inside us, too. They're like our breath. You know how you can see your breath when it is very cold?"

Cecile nodded. She remembered those winter mornings when her

breath was like a white cloud of smoke around her face.

"That reminds us that the fire of life is inside us," Grampa Obomsawin continued. "Those stories are in there, keeping us warm, just as the fire does. And our breath is moist, just like the clouds, which carry the rain. So there is water in the stories, too. The Earth and the Air, the Fire and the Water are our four ancestors, and they all come together to make the stories.

"Long ago, our Creator made the world, and He filled it with stories. Those stories are a gift to us, just like the gift of breath. They're everywhere, all around us. They're inside of us, too, just like that breath we usually can't see. But if we're quiet and we listen, sometimes we'll hear a story."

"So I have stories in me, too, Grampa?"

"You do, indeed. Just keep looking, and sometimes, like on those mornings when you can see your breath, you'll see them. Just keep listening, and you'll hear them, as you do that little wind that is blowing now."

"I'm listening, Grampa," Cecile said.

Grampa Obomsawin smiled. "I'm listening, too," he said.

Then they sat there for a long time, both of them listening for the stories in the wind.

NOTES

Greeting the Sun: The Wampanoag people, whose name means "People of the First Light," live along the Massachusetts coast. Maushop, the giant, is the hero of many Wampanoag stories learned from the Wampanoag elder, Medicine Story.

Thanks to Grandmother Moon: The Mohawk people are one of the five Iroquois Nations. When life on earth began, the Creator told the Iroquois they needed to say a prayer each day to greet and thank everything. "Thanks to Grandmother Moon" is part of that prayer and draws on a version done in Mohawk by Rokwaho and translated by John Stokes and Kanawahienton.

The Moon Basket: The Pawnee are people of the Great Plains. "The Moon Basket" is only one of their many stories about the Sky People—the Moon and the Stars. The work of Alice Fletcher, who recorded many of those tales almost one hundred years ago, was important to me in my version of this story.

The Singing Stars: The Passamaquoddy people, whose name means "place of many fish," live along the coast of Maine. This song refers to a story in which three hunters chase a great bear up into the sky. You can still see the three hunters chasing that bear, the constellation many call The Big Dipper.

The Three Hunters and the Great Bear: The Seneca, the furthest west of the five Iroquois Nations, still live along the Niagara frontier of New York State. Seneca elder and storyteller Marion Miller is one of the contemporary tellers of this story, which was first written down in 1910 by J. N. B. Hewitt.

Firefly Song: The Chippewa people live near the Great Lakes. This lullaby has long been sung to children and has been translated many times since it was recorded by Schoolcraft in 1851.

How Coyote Stole Fire: Most Native nations have a story of how fire was brought to the people. Almost always it is a gift to the people from the birds and animals. This version was learned sixteen years ago from Ted Palmanteer, a Colville writer and artist.

Song of the Earth: The Navajo of the American Southwest have many songs that are part of their rituals for healing. The Navajo word "hozhoni" is usually translated to mean "beauty" or "beautiful," but it also means "balance" and refers to

the natural, healthy state of things. "Life-that-Never-Ends" is another way of saying "Mother Earth," and "Happiness-of-All-Things" is another way of saying "Father Sky." One version of this song was recorded by Natalie Curtis in 1905.

How the Earth Began: The Osage handed down their stories from generation to generation in *wi-gi-es*, poem-stories that the people would all chant together. Those poem-stories contained important lessons for old and young. This story of creation is from an Osage *wi-gi-es*, recorded in 1918 by Francis LaFlesche.

Wihio and Grandfather Rock: The Cheyenne people live in the Great Plains, where their way of life once depended upon the great herds of buffalo. Wihio is their favorite trickster figure, who usually outwits himself.

Inyan, the Rock: This account of creation is adapted from a manuscript completed in 1916 by J. W. Walker, which he based on statements made to him over a period of many years by elderly Oglala Lakotas.

The Shining Mountain: The homelands of the western Abenaki people are the current New England states of Vermont and New Hampshire. A longer version of this traditional song was first written down in English in 1887 by John Reade.

Tacobud, the Mountain That Ate People: The volcanic peaks of the Pacific Northwest are "Mountain People" to Native Americans, who were not surprised by the 1980 eruption of Mount Saint Helens. A version of this story, told by Henry Sicade, a Salish storyteller, can be found in Ella E. Clark's *Indian Legends of the Pacific Northwest*.

Clay Old Man and Clay Old Woman: The people of Cochiti Pueblo, near the Rio Grande River in New Mexico, are famous potters. In 1964, the first clay storyteller dolls were made in Cochiti by Helen Cordero in honor of her grandfather, Santiago Quintana. *Pueblo Stories and Storytellers* (1970) by Mark Bahti contains a fine version of this story.

Talking to the Clay: Michael Simpson's book *Making North American Pottery* (1992) gave me the background information about pottery traditions among Catawba people of North Carolina.

The Cloud-Swallower Giant: This story has been told and retold many times, not just by the Zuni, but by other Pueblo peoples. The first version of it to be published was written down by Frank Hamilton Cushing in *Zuni Folk Tales* (1901).

Papago Rain Song: The Papago people are expert farmers who live in the Sonoran desert lands of Arizona and Mexico. Many of their songs thank the rain and ask it to help them. This version is adapted from a song recorded by Frances Densmore in 1929 in *Papago Music*.

Gluskabe and the Snow Bird: The Abenaki people of the Northeast see many of the forces of nature, especially those having to do with weather, in the shape of great birds. A briefer telling can be found in *Penobscot Tales and Religious Beliefs* by Frank G. Speck (1935).

Song for Going to the Water: This is an original poem adapted from the Cherokee tradition of going to the water, which is described in James Mooney's *Myths of the Cherokee* (1900). "Long Person" means the river itself.

Aglabem's Dam: This version is from the Maliseet people, who live in the Maritime provinces of Canada, north of Maine. A shorter telling can be found in Stith Thompsons's *Tales of the North American Indians* (1929).

Raven and the Tides: The Tshimshian people live along the Pacific coast from southern Alaska through British Columbia. Raven, the best-known trickster figure of that part of the continent, appears in many stories about how things came to be.

How the Prairie Became Ocean: A. L. Kroeber recorded several versions of this creation story from the California coast in his book *Yurok Myths*. This telling draws on the version given to Kroeber by a Yurok elder known as Ann of Espeu.

The Bird Whose Wings Made the Wind: *Legends of the Micmac*, published in 1894 by Silas Rand, contains another version of this widespread story.

Wind Song: *The Pima Indians* (1908) by Russell Frank contains another version of this traditional song.

The Whirlwind of Life: *Holy Wind in Navajo Philosophy* by James McNeley, a book devoted to this concept of the whirlwind of life and breath, is one of my sources for this story.

How Saynday Tried to Marry Whirlwind Girl: Alice Marriott's *Saynday's People* (1947) is a primary source for this story, and the best collection of Saynday stories in print.

How the People Pushed Up the Sky: Sources include Chief William Shelton's *The Story of the Totem Pole* (1935) and Herman Haeberlin's *Mythology of Puget Sound* (1924).

A Song of the Sky: This original poem is partially based on a traditional chief's song recorded by Marius Barbeau in *The Tshimshian, Their Arts and Music*. The chief's song would be sung at a potlatch, a ceremony in which a chief gains status by giving away many presents to everyone.

Bluebird Song from The Night Chant: The Night Chant, one of the great ceremonial chants used for healing the sick, includes more than 360 songs and takes several days to complete. This bluebird song is a very small part of it. This version draws on the Washington Matthews translation "The Night Chant" in *Memoirs of the Museum of Natural History* (1902).

How Songs are Made: Knud Rasmussen's *The Intellectual Culture of the Iglulik Eskimos* (1924) is the source of the quote this poem is based upon.

The Gift of Stories, the Gift of Breath: This is an original story based on discussions with Abenaki elders Maurice Dennis and Cecile Wawanolet.